Suicide
Tragic Choice

Suicide
Tragic Choice

Karen Zeinert

Enslow Publishers, Inc.

40 Industrial Road	PO Box 38
Box 398	Aldershot
Berkeley Heights, NJ 07922	Hants GU12 6BP
USA	UK

http://www.enslow.com

Library of Congress Cataloging-in-Publication Data

Zeinert, Karen.
    Suicide : tragic choice / Karen Zeinert.
        p. cm. — (Issues in focus)
    Summary: Surveys the issue of suicide, including its history,
causes, and psychology.
    ISBN 0-7660-1105-4
    1. Suicide—Juvenile literature. 2. Suicide—Prevention—Juvenile
literature. 3. Suicide victims—Psychology—Juvenile literature.
[1. Suicide.] I. Title. II. Series: Issues in focus (Hillside, N.J.)
    HV6545.Z43 1999
    362.28—dc21   98-43807
                                            CIP
                                            AC
Printed in the United States of America

10 9 8 7 6 5 4 3 2 1

To Our Readers: All Internet addresses in this book were active and
appropriate when we went to press. Any comments or suggestions can be
sent by e-mail to Comments@enslow.com or to the address on the back
cover.

Illustration Credits: AP/Wide World Photos, pp. 9, 25, 84, 92,
101; Courtesy of Rick Balin/Appleton Medical Center, p. 73;
Dover Pictorial Archives, pp. 16, 19, 20; Courtesy of John A.
Zeinert, pp. 31, 32, 38, 42, 46, 49, 60.

Cover Illustration: Courtesy of Skjold Photographs.

Contents

1

Death in the Headlines

On March 26, 1997, Officer Robert Brunk of the San Diego County sheriff's department entered a Rancho Santa Fe mansion, where he found the remains of thirty-nine people who had committed suicide. After coming to grips with the horrible scene before him, Brunk called in medical examiners to try to determine exactly what had happened in the mansion. Eventually the examiners announced that twenty-one women and eighteen men, ranging in age from twenty-six to seventy-two and all members of a religious group known as Heaven's Gate, had died in shifts. Fifteen had donned clean clothes and black sneakers before taking their lives on March 23. Another fifteen, after covering the first corpses with diamond-shaped purple shrouds, followed suit the next day. The rest committed suicide on March 25. Needless to say, this mass suicide made headlines in newspapers all across the country. These deaths were also discussed in feature articles in numerous news magazines such as *Newsweek* and *Time*, both of which pictured the group's leader, Marshall Herff Applewhite, on their covers.

On April 8, 1994, twenty-seven-year-old Kurt Cobain, an incredibly successful rock star and leader of the group Nirvana, took his own life. At least two teens in America imitated his suicide shortly after, shooting themselves in the head.[1] Three years later, in May 1997, two French girls, ages twelve and thirteen, copied Cobain's death. These suicides also made the news.[2]

In November 1997, nineteen-year-old Moshe Pergament, a quiet college student, purposely drove too fast on the Long Island Expressway in order to get arrested. When police finally stopped him, he waved a toy gun in the air and ignored all warnings to drop his weapon. Instead, Pergament began to advance toward the officers. They fired their revolvers, fatally wounding the teen. Later, police found a note in Pergament's car addressed to "the officer who shot me." The note said in part: "Officer, It was a plan. I'm sorry to get you involved. I just needed to die."[3] Another headline-making story followed. This time it discussed "suicide-by-cop," which at that time was a rare event.[4]

One month later, on December 20, 1997, the media was once again busy covering another suicide. This time Anthony DeCulit, a postal employee in Milwaukee, Wisconsin, shot and killed a coworker with whom he had feuded. DeCulit then wounded a supervisor before killing himself.[5]

These suicides made the news because something

Kurt Cobain (right) and his fellow grunge rockers won MTV's award for the best alternative video in September 1993. Six months later, Cobain killed himself.

about the deaths—the sheer number of deceased, for example—made them unusual. They sickened and yet, at the same time, somehow fascinated the public. These deaths also reminded Americans that suicide is a common event in the United States.

Suicide Occurs Often

According to official reports, about thirty-five thousand Americans kill themselves each year. Experts believe that the real number may be as high as one hundred thousand, though, because many accidents may actually be suicides in disguise.[6] These numbers may not seem great, but killing oneself is so common that most of us at some point in our lives will lose a friend, a neighbor, a classmate, or a relative to suicide. In fact, in the time that it takes to read this book, several teens will try to kill themselves and one will be successful. Not only is a life forever lost, but also the anguish and despair that survivors—friends and relatives—feel can forever affect their lives, greatly increasing the effect of a single bullet or a dozen pills. So each time a suicide is reported, most Americans rail against taking one's own life.

Suicide Is Controversial

Yet at the same time, there was—and still is—a strong demand for *Final Exit*, a how-to suicide manual. This book, written in 1991 by Derek Humphry, actually topped *The New York Times* "Best Seller List" for many months and remained immensely popular in the years that followed. This contradiction—condemning suicide and yet eagerly snatching up a book about how to do it—is an example of Americans' mixed attitudes about the practice of taking one's own life.

The following pages, which are meant to help you form your own opinions regarding suicide, explore a variety of topics that surround this complex and controversial issue. Is suicide a modern phenomenon? If not, how has it been dealt with in the past? Which people are most likely to take their own lives? For what reason will they do so? How can we recognize—and help—people who might be thinking about ending their lives? Is there such a thing as an acceptable suicide? And finally, how can we help the survivors of the deceased when a suicide takes place?

2

Suicide in the Past

Suicide is not a new phenomenon. In fact, a written statement about taking one's own life was made more than four thousand years ago by a lonely man in ancient Egypt. He wrote a poem, seven pages long, in which he explained why he wanted to die that very day. He said, in part:

> To whom shall I speak today?
> Brothers are mean,
> One goes to strangers for affection . . .
>
> To whom shall I speak today?
> I am burdened with grief
> For lack of a [friend] . . .

Death is before me today
[Like] a sick man's recovery,
Like going outdoors after confinement . . .

Death is before me today
Like a man's longing to see his home
When he has spent many years in captivity.[1]

Whether this man committed suicide is not certain. What is certain is that taking one's life was not uncommon in ancient times. One Egyptian writer claimed that so many of his countrymen were killing themselves by jumping into the Nile River that the crocodiles were becoming fat from feasting on their corpses.[2]

Suicide in Other Ancient Civilizations

Egypt was only one of a number of ancient cultures in which suicide took place. Many suicides occurred in Greece, India, Japan, and Africa.

However, how ancient civilizations regarded suicide varied greatly. Some accepted it under certain circumstances. In Greece, for example, committing suicide was acceptable when one's health failed or when one was facing scandal and shame. Anyone contemplating suicide had only to convince local authorities that his or her death was a reasonable act. If the applicant was persuasive, he or she was given a carefully measured dose of poison to drink, which was guaranteed to bring about a quick death.

Suicide was also acceptable in India. When their masters died, slaves were expected to kill themselves to show unswerving loyalty to their owners.

Likewise, a widow was expected to throw herself onto the burning pyre that cremated her husband's corpse, in effect burning herself alive. This practice, called suttee, continued well into the 1800s but is now outlawed.

Other ancient civilizations accepted suicide only during difficult times. When famine struck, Eskimos hoped that older citizens would voluntarily end their lives so that younger people might have a better chance to survive. The Japanese expected military leaders who had behaved in a cowardly fashion to kill themselves. In addition, some ancient civilizations accepted suicide, even mass suicide, in order to avoid enslavement. For example, in A.D. 73, approximately 960 Jews who were besieged at Masada killed themselves rather than be taken prisoner by the Romans.

On the other hand, some ancient civilizations were appalled by suicide under any circumstances. The Baganda, who still live in what is now Uganda, believed that the spirit of a suicide victim suffered so much from the victim's traumatic death that it could not rest. Instead, it wandered about, angry and unhappy, seeking someone to punish. As a result, the bodies of suicide victims were burned in hopes of killing the spirit or wounding it to such a degree that it could do no harm.

Also, not everyone in an ancient society that approved of suicide accepted that society's generally held belief. In Greece, for instance, two famous philosophers, Plato and Aristotle, eventually spoke out against the practice. Plato thought that suicide was a cowardly act. In his opinion, Greeks had to learn to deal with their problems, not run away from them, an idea that is often repeated today. Aristotle believed that killing oneself was socially irresponsible because it deprived society of a vitally needed worker.

Christianity and Suicide

Eventually, most religious leaders in the ancient world, especially those associated with Christianity, considered doing away with oneself an appalling practice. One of the most outspoken leaders against suicide was St. Augustine, who lived in the fourth and fifth centuries. Augustine argued, as had Plato and Aristotle, that suicide was socially irresponsible. In addition, Augustine believed that suicide was a form of murder, self-murder, for which there was no forgiveness. If the act was successful, the perpetrators could not ask for a pardon afterward; if they were truly sorry for killing themselves, they would not commit suicide in the first place. Only God, Augustine insisted, should decide when someone dies. Furthermore, Augustine added, life was a gift from God, and to reject this gift was to reject God. As a result, Christians who committed suicide could expect to spend eternity in hell.

When St. Augustine's arguments failed to put an end to suicides, the Roman Catholic Church, and later many Protestant churches throughout Europe, tried another tactic to make potential self-murderers think twice before killing themselves. Anyone who committed suicide would be denied a Christian burial. This punishment not only emphasized the

Christian martyrs welcomed death no matter how awful the execution might be. This old woodcut illustrates one of the popular methods used—being burned at the stake.

seriousness of the crime, but also would humiliate grieving family members who survived the deceased.

More Shame

But no matter how hard religious leaders tried to cut the suicide rates by threatening people with eternal damnation and the denial of a proper burial, the practice continued. So a new punishment was devised in some communities in England and, later, in the American colonies: The corpse of a self-murderer would be publicly desecrated. Although it is unclear whether religious leaders or their followers performed the deed, someone drove a stake through the heart of the deceased and cut off the hand that was thought to have committed the suicide. The corpse was then buried under a pile of rocks at a prominent intersection near town to remind passersby about what happened to self-murderers. Some historians believe that burying these corpses near an intersection was also symbolic: The deceased had a choice, and he or she had taken the wrong road in life. Sometimes the deceased were stripped naked and dragged through the streets before being dumped outside of town, where vultures and crows would eventually pick the bones clean.

Suicide and the Law

Still the practice of suicide continued. So government officials became involved. In England, Parliament passed laws that made it possible for local officials to claim all worldly goods left by anyone who took his or her life. Now, not only would the deceased's soul endure eternal damnation, his or her corpse be desecrated, *and* the survivors of the deceased be publicly humiliated, the survivors would lose their inheritance as well.

New laws also made it possible to arrest and punish anyone who survived a suicide attempt. Ironically, because suicide was listed as a serious crime, it was not unusual for officials to hang those who had tried to kill themselves. Although these laws were not strictly enforced after the 1700s, they remained on the books well into the twentieth century.

A Change in Attitude

While the Church and the government argued that suicide was a sin and a crime, a very different attitude took hold among some young artists and writers in the eighteenth and nineteenth centuries. Although death had long been a popular subject in art, suicide had seldom been portrayed, in part because it was viewed with such horror and disgust. Now young painters, novelists, and poets began to look upon suicide as both a romantic act and a dramatic way to make a statement.

The work that these artists and writers created was quite different from what the public had come to expect. In literature, for example, fictional heroes were sensitive men whose talents and works were ignored or laughed at by a hostile and ignorant public. Rather than change their standards to what the public wanted, the heroes killed themselves. Fictional heroines were often pictured as beautiful, broken-hearted lovers who had been rejected by callous cads or kept from their true love by cruel foes. Sometimes authors wrote stories about ill-fated lovers who committed suicide so that they might be together forever. In all cases, the dead were mourned with great fervor, usually by the same public, lovers, and foes who had rejected or hurt them.

The works of the Romantic writers, as they were eventually called, had a tremendous effect. One of

Christian leaders warned followers that anyone who committed suicide would face an eternity in hell. This is one artist's version of hell, published in 1688.

the best examples of a Romantic writer's impact is the work of German writer Johann Goethe. One of his most popular novels, *The Sorrows of Young Werther*, is a series of letters written by Werther. Through these letters, Werther tells a dear friend about his love for Charlotte, a beautiful woman who

Death, shown hovering over the artist and his model, was a popular subject with painters and writers in the 1600s. In the 1700s, artists began to portray suicide as a romantic gesture.

marries a man named Albert. Werther eventually kills himself rather than live without his love. Many young men throughout Europe, apparently unhappy in love as well, were taken by this sad story. They began to imitate Werther's dress—a blue coat and yellow vest—and his exaggerated sensitivity to events around him. Some even committed suicide. When they killed themselves, they were said to be suffering from Wertheritis.

In France, the idea of suicide became so popular at one point that some young adults formed suicide clubs. However, even though members claimed that they wanted to kill themselves, few actually did.

New Ideas About Suicide

While some writers hailed suicide, a few doctors and sociologists began to take a scientific look at the practice. Eventually called suicidologists, they rejected the popular ideas that suicide was a sin or a crime or a romantic gesture. Some suicidologists believed that suicide was the result of mental illness. Others argued that physical causes, such as lesions on the brain, brought about suicide. A third group believed that social causes—poverty, for example—encouraged people to end their lives. Unable to reach an agreement about what brought about such deaths, during the next hundred years suicidologists became embroiled in heated debates and gathered information to support their arguments.

But even after a century of study, many questions still remain. So, suicidologists continue to examine

The Sorrows of Young Werther

Johann Goethe's book about Werther and his unrequited love for Charlotte was very popular, though critics claimed it promoted suicide. Below are several excerpts from the book, a series of letters written by Werther:

August 21

In vain I stretch out my arms towards her. . . . Tears flow from my oppressed heart; and, bereft of all comfort, I weep over my dark future.

September 3

I sometimes cannot understand how another can love her so, dare love her, when I love nothing in this world so completely, so devotedly, as I love her, when she is my only thought, and I have nothing but her in the whole world.

November 26

I often say to myself, "You alone are wretched; all others are happy; no one has ever been tormented like you."

December 20

My mind is made up, Charlotte: I am resolved to die!. . . When you read this, my dearest, the cool grave will cover the stiff remains of that restless and unhappy man who, in the last moments of his life, knows no greater bliss than to [write to] you! . . . All is silent around me, and my soul is calm. . . . I wish to be buried in the clothes I wear at present; you have touched them. . . . The clock strikes twelve. So be it! Charlotte! Charlotte, farewell, farewell![3]

case after case. They sift through a growing pile of statistics, interview survivors of those who ended their own lives, and study the lives of the deceased in detail. Like detectives, they hope to find answers—lots of answers—that will help them, and us, better understand suicide.

3

Who Commits Suicide?

When suicidologists first set out about one hundred years ago to gather information to determine who committed suicide, why they did so, and how they did it, they encountered serious problems. Because most people thought that a self-inflicted death was a mortal sin, many friends and relatives of those who had committed suicide were too ashamed to talk.

Second, because suicide was regarded as shameful, criminal, and sinful, and because life insurance companies often failed to pay if a death was declared self-inflicted, the few survivors who agreed to be interviewed usually tried to hide the truth. Many insisted that a suicide was really an accident. This greatly affected the records, making suicide appear to be less of a problem than it really was.

To further complicate the issue, if survivors agreed to tell what had happened, different suicidologists used different ways to express their findings. This made it very difficult to compare studies and draw conclusions.

Suicide Rate

To make their information about who committed suicide more useful, suicidologists eventually decided to use a standard suicide rate. Interviewers would determine how many people in a particular group—white men or African-American women, for instance—had committed suicide in a certain year. Then, to make comparisons between groups easier, results would be expressed not in total numbers of deaths, because different groups had different populations, but in the number of suicides per one hundred thousand members.

Continued Difficulties

Although having a standardized rate today makes comparisons easier, suicidologists still struggle to get accurate statistics for these rates. This difficulty is due, in part, to the fact that old attitudes about suicide continue to exist and, therefore, some suicides are not reported. So, the totals are not always accurate; in reality, they may be much higher. Even so, the rates help experts identify trends and name some of the groups most at risk to kill themselves.

Suicide Rates in the United States

Suicide rates are reported regularly by the United States National Center for Health Statistics, usually using information from the Centers for Disease Control and Prevention (CDC). Unless otherwise noted, the rates and numbers given in this chapter are from the latest reports by the CDC.[1] These reports are based on 1995 data—it takes several years to gather, analyze, and publish information— which was updated in January 1998.

According to the CDC, the suicide rate in the United States is 11.0. This means that approximately

Some Americans are more likely than others to commit suicide. This chapter helps identify those groups most at risk.

eleven out of every one hundred thousand Americans killed themselves in 1995. This number has not varied greatly for several years, sometimes rising to 12 or falling to a little over 10. (For comparison's sake, Russia's rate—again, based on 1995 statistics— is 44.4. It is the highest in the world, whereas Italy's rate of 7.1 is one of the lowest.)

To put suicide into perspective, experts often compare the number of self-inflicted deaths with other causes of death in America. In 1995, approximately thirty-one thousand Americans took their own lives. This accounts for 1.3 percent of all deaths in the United States. In comparison, 32 percent died from heart disease, 23 percent died from cancer, and 6.8 percent died from cerebrovascular disease (stroke), the three leading causes of death in the United States.

Male and Female

When suicidologists first looked at years of data, one of the things they noted was that males were five times more likely than females to commit suicide. This is still true today. Out of the thirty-one thousand Americans who killed themselves in 1995, twenty-five thousand were boys and men. The suicide rate for males is 19.8, while the rate for females is 3.8.

The vast difference between these rates does not mean that females don't try to kill themselves. In fact, girls and women are three times more likely than males to try to commit suicide. They just aren't as effective in their efforts.

Age

A significant difference between the sexes in regard to suicide was not the only pattern to emerge. According to suicidologists, members of certain age groups are more likely than others to commit suicide.

Few records of attempted or completed suicides made by children younger than five years of age have been recorded. But even though records do not exist, suicidologists believe that some children only three years old have tried to take their own lives.

Records for the next age group, children ages five to fourteen, have been kept and they are added to each year. These records indicate that this group has a very low suicide rate: .9, or less than one death per one hundred thousand children. The rate for boys is 1.2, and the rate for girls is .5. Although these rates would not seem to demand attention, they represent a significant increase in self-inflicted deaths in this group since 1950. In fact, the number of suicides just among ten- to fourteen-year-olds has increased 300 percent.

According to the CDC's statistics, the next age bracket, ages fifteen to twenty-four, loses about five thousand members each year to suicide. The rate for this group is 13.6 (23.4 for males, 3.7 for females). Suicide is the third leading cause of death for teens, just behind automobile accidents and murder. But because suicidologists believe that many single-car automobile accidents are not accidents at all but rather suicides in disguise, self-inflicted deaths may very well be the leading cause of death for this group.[2]

The suicide rate is even higher for adults, ages twenty-five to forty-four. The rate for men is 24.8; for women, 5.9. This represents more than twelve thousand deaths. Accidents of all kinds—again, some of which are single-car crashes and may in fact not be accidents—and death from AIDS, a disease that destroys a person's immune system, are the major causes of death for this group, taking more than thirty-two thousand lives each year.

Americans ages forty-five to sixty-four also have a higher than average suicide rate, 14 per 100,000 people. The rate for men is 22.1, and the rate for women is 6.4. Even so, suicide is the tenth leading cause of death for this group. Cancer, which claims more than 130,000 lives per year in this age bracket, heads the list.

The last group, people over age sixty-five are, like children ages five to fourteen, increasingly taking their own lives. Since 1980, the number of elderly Americans who have chosen to die has grown. In 1980, the suicide rate for this group was 17.6. In 1988 it reached 20.9.[3] The most recent statistics indicate that the overall rate is 22.

Racial and Ethnic Groups

Until twenty-five years ago, Americans were classified as white and nonwhite (African Americans,

American Indians, and Asians, for example), for almost all studies. So until the mid-1970s, it was very difficult to determine whether one particular racial or ethnic group was more likely to commit suicide than another. Once Americans were separated, however, significant differences became apparent.

The rate for all whites was—and still is—approximately 13, a little bit above the national average. Even so, this group, which is made up of millions of Americans, accounts for most of the suicides committed in the United States. Of the thirty-one thousand Americans who recently took their own lives, twenty-eight thousand were white. The vast majority of these suicides, twenty-two thousand, were committed by young adult men, ages twenty to thirty-four, and males over the age of sixty-five. In fact, one of the groups most at risk consists of white males over the age of eighty-five. This group has a suicide rate of 68.2.

On the other hand, African Americans experience a low suicide rate. Whereas twenty-eight thousand whites took their lives in 1995, only twenty-three hundred African Americans did so. Almost half these deaths occurred among African Americans ages twenty to thirty-four, whose suicide rate is about 12. The rate then drops among older adult African Americans, and it is less than 7 for elderly African Americans.

How much longer rates will remain low for African Americans is not certain. Recent studies indicate that some groups are at great risk. For example, the rate for suicides among African-American teens has doubled since 1980. At that time, the suicide rate for African Americans ages ten to nineteen was 2.1 Today it is 4.5. Among whites the same age, the rate increased from 5.4 to 6.4.

As early as 1970, a few researchers noted that American Indians had a high suicide rate, 21.6 per one hundred thousand. By the late 1980s, the rate had climbed to 29.[4] The greatest number of suicides occurred among male teens and young adults. Today, the rate is still higher than the national average.

To date, only a few, limited suicide studies have been made about Hispanic Americans. So far, these studies indicate that the suicide rate for this group is about 9. Almost 70 percent of those who took their own lives did so before they reached the age of forty.[5]

Location

Suicidologists even study location, wondering whether the suicide rate varies from state to state, region to region, or between large cities and rural areas. Their current findings indicate that Nevada has the highest suicide rate, twice that of the national average. Data also show that all but one of the states that have higher than average suicide rates are located west of the Mississippi River. These states are Alaska, Arizona, California, Colorado, Florida, Montana, New Mexico, Oregon, and Wyoming.

When suicidologists divide the nation into sections, they also note significant differences. The average rate for the thirteen western states is 14.1. The states with the lowest suicide rates are found in the Northeast (8.6) and in the Midwest (11.4). The rate in the South is 13.1.

For years, it was believed that people in small cities and rural areas committed suicide less often than people who lived in big cities. This was true sixty years ago when the average suicide rate in large cities was 17 and the rate in rural areas was 11. By 1991, though, there was little difference in the rate between city dwellers and their country cousins.[6]

For many years, people who lived in large cities were more likely to commit suicide than people who lived in rural areas.

The suicide rate in rural areas has increased dramatically over the years.

Religious Beliefs

Over the years interviewers studied various religious groups as well. Because suicide had long been viewed with horror and disgust by many religious leaders, members of Christian denominations as well as members of the Jewish faith, interviewers were not surprised to learn that these groups had lower than average suicide rates in the past. Although some suicidologists believe that this trend continues today, this is difficult to prove. Death certificates do not have to indicate the deceased's religion.

Whereas some religious groups have been known for their opposition to suicide, others have committed mass suicide. Almost all the members of the group Heaven's Gate (Chapter 1) killed themselves when their leader told them to do so. Even some former members followed suit days after. One of the most famous mass suicides took place in 1978, when more than nine hundred members of a religious cult died in Jonestown, Guyana, in South America. This group, consisting mostly of Americans, was led by Jim Jones, who had moved his followers from California to Guyana in 1977.

Sexual Orientation

Finally, suicidologists explored the issue of sexual orientation. How, they wondered, did the suicide rate for heterosexuals compare with that of homosexuals? Interviewers soon discovered that it was nearly impossible to determine a rate for homosexual

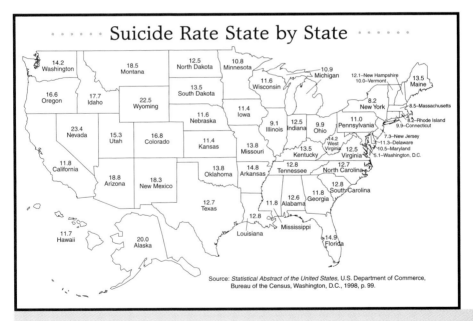

Suicide Rate State by State

14.2 Washington	18.5 Montana	12.5 North Dakota

Source: *Statistical Abstract of the United States*, U.S. Department of Commerce, Bureau of the Census, Washington, D.C., 1998, p. 99.

The numbers represent how many people out of 100,000 killed themselves in one calendar year.

Americans, because many hid their sexual orientation out of fear of persecution.

The most extensive study to date was ordered by the United States Department of Health and Human Services. In *A Report of the Secretary's Task Force on Youth Suicide*, interviewers concluded that an estimated 30 percent of completed youth suicides were committed by homosexuals.[7] This 1989 report was very controversial. Opponents claimed that the suicide rate was greatly exaggerated in order to gain public support and sympathy for the gay community. However, statistics from studies done by the University of Minnesota Adolescent Health Program in Minneapolis and the Los Angeles Suicide Prevention Center, both of which were completed before this report, also showed that homosexuals were at high risk.[8]

Because so much controversy surrounds the issue of homosexuality and suicide, funds for more studies are limited. Even so, some suicidologists are determined to study this group in greater detail.

Why?

Once suicidologists had statistics in hand and could identify the people most at risk, they set out to identify the reasons behind so many deaths. What makes more than thirty thousand Americans choose death over life every year? Why are some groups more likely to end their lives than others?

4

Why?

The most often asked question after someone has committed suicide is "Why?" Although no two deaths are exactly alike, when suicidologists study notes left behind by the deceased and interview survivors, some similarities appear. Most experts believe that suicide is seldom the result of a single cause. Rather it is a combination of some of the following that overwhelm an individual: depression; drug and alcohol abuse; social, religious, and sexual issues; and wishful thinking.

Depression

Although Americans are bombarded daily by advertisements that picture nothing

35

but happy people—at least while using the right product—very few of us actually sing and shout for joy every day. In reality, life has its up and downs. For most people, the downs are short, perhaps a week long at best. We may feel more tired then, a little sad, and less sociable than usual. Often such spells, sometimes called the blues, occur when something is bothering us. They are normal and commonplace, but one's first experience with them can be a little unsettling.

But if the blues become more intense or last for more than two to three weeks, it is cause for concern. The blues may actually be depression, which requires medical attention and counseling, and according to suicidologists, plays a major role in at least 70 percent of all suicides.

Typical cases of depression are easy to spot. Depressed people

- cry easily and often;
- have little or no energy;
- experience a dramatic change in sleeping habits;
- believe that the future is hopeless;
- believe that they are worthless;
- refuse to take care of themselves properly, eating too little or too much, ignoring personal hygiene.

But not all depression cases are typical, and, therefore, some are not diagnosed correctly. First of all, sufferers sometimes mask, or hide, their depression. Instead of withdrawing or crying, they may act out, taking great risks, seeking punishment because they feel worthless. Young children may repeatedly throw tantrums, for example, and teens might resort to fighting or taking drugs.

Another factor that has allowed some depression cases to go unrecognized is an old-fashioned belief about who gets depressed. Depression is more common than generally realized—one out of every four Americans will probably suffer from it sometime during his or her lifetime—and anyone, young or old, can be a depression victim. Still, some counselors believe that children, who are supposedly enjoying the best years of their lives, can't become depressed. Instead, deeply unhappy children—especially teenagers—are thought to be going through a difficult stage. Also, depression in elderly Americans is sometimes thought to be little more than part of the natural aging process. In both cases, the depression may be ignored and go untreated.

Causes of Depression

Psychologists and psychiatrists have studied depression for many years. In the process they have discovered several factors that can bring about depression so severe that sufferers may just want to die.

One cause of depression is significant loss; the death of someone who was dearly loved, for example. It is normal to feel distressed when someone we love dies or a special friendship ends. It is also normal to

Depression plays a major role in suicide.

feel blue if we lose our job or fail to achieve an important goal.

Whereas many people recover from depression on their own, some cannot adjust to their loss without help. Those who lacked confidence and self-esteem before their loss sometimes believe that life is hopeless without their loved one or that they are worthless because they have failed. This is especially true if someone pinned everything on a particular person or a certain goal. The thinking goes something like this: *If . . . was alive, if . . . would still be my friend, if I had won, . . . I would be a worthy person. Now without . . . , I am nothing.*

Another possible cause of depression, and a cause of low self-esteem as well, is abuse: repeated physical assaults and verbal attacks. These undermine a person's sense of worth. This is especially true if the abuse is meted out by the very people who are supposed to love the victim—parents, siblings, spouses, and in the case of elder abuse, children. Victims may assume that there must be a reason that they were attacked, that they either did something wrong or that there is something wrong with them. This can lead victims to feel guilty and ashamed and to believe that they are unloveable.

The results of one kind of physical abuse, sexual assaults, were highlighted in a special study conducted by Dr. Angela Diaz, chief of adolescent medicine at Mount Sinai Medical Center in New York City. Her study found that girls who had been repeatedly sexually assaulted had experienced dramatic mood swings, chronic tiredness, and long-term insomnia, all typical signs of depression. More than 80 percent of the victims thought about committing suicide, and half of them tried to do so, often more than once.[1]

Verbal abuse can also cause depression. Children sometimes chant: "Sticks and stones may break my bones, but names will never hurt me," when taunted by a classmate. Although they may pretend to believe these words, name calling and insults hurt more than most people want to admit. Those who experience repeated put-downs may end up feeling worthless.

Often these feelings are long-lived. One thirty-nine-year-old adult who had been told as a child that she was so fat that she was a "cow" said, "I think part of my weight and eating disorder problems are from believing that I was a cow. . . . I have a low self-image and self-worth, and at one time they were so low, I didn't believe anyone would care if I was alive or not."[2]

Victims of abuse experience great anger at their tormentors. But because it is often dangerous for these victims, particularly young children, to express their rage, they "swallow" it, aiming it at themselves. They belittle themselves and dwell upon their mistakes, often calling themselves clumsy or stupid. Anger directed inward is enough to cause serious depression.

Depression may also be caused by physical abnormalities. Drs. Neal D. Ryan and Joaquim Puig-Antich, who work with suicidal adolescents, noted that teens who tried to kill themselves had very low levels of the growth hormone produced by the pituitary gland. Other studies have indicated that some people who have become depressed and have committed suicide had a low level of 5-hydroxyindoleacetic acid, 5HIAA for short, in their brain. This chemical is a byproduct of serotonin, which is believed to regulate mood.[3]

The connection between a shortage of 5HIAA and suicide was first discovered in 1975 by Swedish psychiatrist Marie Asberg. She found that 66 percent of the people who committed suicide recently had had low levels of 5HIAA.[4]

Since then, more studies have been done. To date, these studies indicate that some, but not all, people who have little 5HIAA in their system become depressed. So far, tests have only been conducted on adults, and it is not clear whether children who commit suicide also have a lower than normal amount of 5HIAA in their bodies.

Other Factors—Drug and Alcohol Abuse

Another cause of suicide is drug and alcohol abuse. Although not all people who abuse drugs and alcohol will commit suicide, the more they abuse these substances, the more likely it is that they will intentionally kill themselves. The suicide rate for abusers is 60 per 100,000, five times greater than that of the general population.[5]

Those who abuse drugs and alcohol do so to escape their pain or to feel better about themselves, and many may already be depressed. Drug abuse often becomes a source of conflict between the user and his or her loved ones. Also, abuse can cause users to withdraw into a make-believe world. As a result, they fail in school or lose their jobs. Conflict and failure can lead to depression or increase it if it already exists. In addition, although alcohol may make a person feel temporarily happy, in the long run alcohol is a depressant. When it is abused by people suffering from depression, it can further depress them, increasing feelings of helplessness and hopelessness.

Drug and alcohol abuse also reduces inhibitions, making it possible for users to take risks that they would avoid if they were sober—driving recklessly, for instance. Each year more than forty-four thousand people die in automobile accidents. Records show that half these accidents involve alcohol or drugs.[6] Experts wonder whether some of these

Drugs and alcohol are often abused by depressed people in order to escape from their emotional pain. Depression and substance abuse make a deadly combination.

deaths were deliberate or examples of risk-taking that turned deadly.

Still, not all people who were depressed and abused drugs and alcohol committed suicide. So suicidologists continue to look for yet another factor or two. What else, they wonder, plays a role in thirty thousand deaths a year?

Social Issues

One of the things that suicidologists study is history. Were there times when the suicide rate varied greatly from the average? If so, what was happening then? Suicidologists noted that the rate rose during times of great economic hardships—the Great Depression in the 1930s, for example, when more than one fourth of all workers could not find a job. However, when America was in peril and needed every hand possible—World War II, for instance—the suicide rate decreased. Also, suicidologists noticed that during times of social upheaval, when society in general was undergoing great change, Americans were more likely to commit suicide.

Among the many changes that Americans are experiencing today is increased mobility. More than one fourth of the population moves every five years. This results in the loss of friendships and close ties to extended family members, grandparents, and aunts and uncles. Sometimes moving from one place to another can be a "triggering event," the final straw, for someone who is already depressed. Suicidologists believe that deeply depressed children may take their own lives rather than face living in a strange new world.

Mobility also plays a role in the high suicide rate in certain states. Senior citizens are one of the most mobile groups in America, and it is not uncommon for older people in the colder climates in the United States to move to Florida or to the Southwest when they retire. Often, though, when a spouse dies, the survivor feels isolated, far away from relatives and lifelong friends. If the survivor is also experiencing serious health problems, he or she may decide to commit suicide.

Interestingly enough, when older Americans want to kill themselves, they are very effective at doing so. The ratio of attempted suicides to actual suicides among all Americans is 10:1, that is, out of every ten Americans who try to kill themselves, one will actually succeed. For young adults, the ratio is 100:1. For adults over the age of fifty-five, the ratio, according to one study, is 1:1.[7] The large number of older adults in Florida and some of the western states and their ability to kill themselves so effectively accounts for, in part, the higher suicide rate in these states. It also explains why the rate for older Americans is so much higher than that of teenagers.

Another social issue that plays a role in suicide is stress, especially in the home. Many families undergo great changes over the years in addition to moving about. Divorce—today more than half of all marriages end in divorce—and remarriage are now common. Children may find themselves in the middle of a bitter divorce fight or living with stepsiblings, as well as a stepparent, none of whom they particularly like. The loss of the ideal of living happily with both natural parents is difficult for some children to accept, and they mourn their loss. Although divorce is not the only factor in the growing suicide rate among adolescents, it is a factor that has to be considered. An estimated 70 percent of children who commit suicide come from divorced families.[8]

Divorce and remarriage are only two things that cause stress in the American home. Sometimes there is little communication in families, and children feel isolated and unwanted. In other homes, children may be given a lot of attention and pressured to move to the head of their class, to be a star even if they aren't able to do so. Worse yet, parents in such homes may show signs of affection only when a goal is met. The results in both cases are misunderstanding, conflict, and possibly thoughts of suicide. In a recent study, Michael Peck and Robert Litman discovered that approximately 90 percent of young people who were suicidal believed that their parents did not understand them. A majority, 66 percent, of those who committed suicide had long been on bad terms with family members.[9]

Cultural Issues

Cultural issues also play a role in suicide, putting some groups more at risk than others. American Indians, for example, most of whom live on reservations, have one of the highest suicide rates in America. They also have serious alcohol and drug abuse problems and overwhelming poverty. The majority of suicides in this group are committed by teens and young adults who are trying to decide how to live out their lives. If they remain on the reservation, where few jobs exist, their futures will be difficult. If they leave the reservation, they leave their friends, family, and ancestral homeland—a painful decision at best.

In contrast, African Americans have long had a low suicide rate. That's why the increase in the last few years in the number of suicides among African-American teenagers is so upsetting. Experts at the

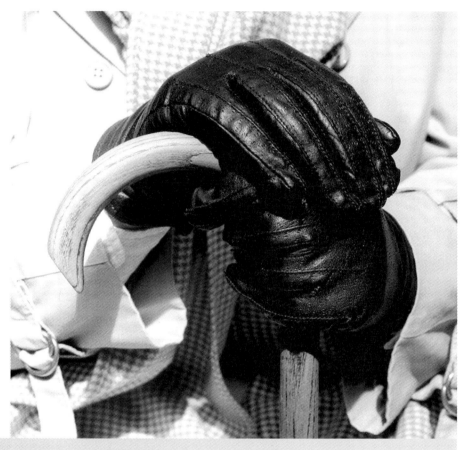

The suicide rate among the elderly is soaring.

Centers for Disease Control and Prevention believe that this increase is due to stress. Many young African Americans face extreme pressure from parents to achieve in school. Some in the African-American community regard this as trying to be more like whites, and, therefore, unacceptable. So, young African Americans who excel may find themselves cut off from old friends. The result is a lot of conflict and stress.[10]

On the other hand, whereas the suicide rate is rising for African-American teens, the rate for elderly African Americans remains extremely low, far below that of older whites. Suicidologists believe that several factors are involved in this low rate. First, older African Americans, especially women, have long played an important role in their families, many of which are headed by single mothers. Grandparents are needed; they are expected to help raise grandchildren. Also, most elderly African Americans have experienced difficult times throughout their lives. They know how to cope with life and can handle crises that might bring others low.[11]

Unlike elderly African-Americans citizens, older whites, especially males who have had very success-ful careers, have a high suicide rate. Suicidologists speculate that these people kill themselves because they no longer feel needed, nor do they command the respect that they once had. If these men are widow-ers, they are at an even greater risk of killing themselves.[12]

Religious Groups

Some religious groups isolate themselves, setting up separate communities and establishing a new belief system. The result can be deadly. Some of these groups tend to spend their time preparing for a future paradise. Sometimes they decide to die to reach heaven as soon as possible, or they anticipate a particular moment when they believe that they are supposed to die. Heaven's Gate followers, for example, believed that the appearance of the Hale-Bopp comet was a sign indicating that all was ready for them. They thought that a spaceship that would take them to paradise was hidden in the wake of the comet. All they had to do to board this unseen ship was to shed their "containers," their bodies, so that their spirits could rise toward the comet.[13]

Perhaps the most famous mass suicide was that of the People's Temple—Jim Jones's followers in South America. Jones had several encounters with the law in Guyana, just as he had in the United States. When authorities began a formal investigation of some strange—and probably illegal—activities in the religious community, Jones panicked and ordered his followers, who had routinely practiced suicide drills, to kill themselves. After being told that they would be together in paradise, Jones's followers were given a drink laced with poison. Although the total number of deaths was over nine hundred, not all agreed to kill themselves. Some of the dead were murdered. Jones hoped to eliminate all members so that no followers would be left behind to talk about him. However, a few managed to escape.

Sexual Issues

Sexual identity can also play a role in suicide. Homosexuality is not widely accepted in the United States. In fact, in some circles it is looked upon as a sin. So being gay in America is not easy. Among

Some American Indians live on reservations, such as this one, in Arizona. Although often surrounded by dramatic beauty, American Indians have one of the highest suicide rates in the United States.

homosexuals—who had made public their sexual preference—interviewed for various studies during the 1980s and early 1990s, more than half reported being physically and verbally abused. Almost all in this group had been insulted prior to being beaten, robbed, or raped. To make matters worse, former friends refused to be seen with them. And a number of homosexuals had been cut off by their families when they told their parents and siblings about their sexual orientation.[14]

These same studies indicated that teenage homosexuals are more likely to commit suicide than older gays. It is during the teen years that young people first become aware of their sexual preferences. It is also the time in life when young adults are trying to become more independent. As they gradually sever ties with their parents, teens seek a new support system—their peers. In order to do this, teens try to fit in, to be like everyone else. Homosexuals are different from the majority, and as a result, if they are identified, they are not always well accepted. On the other hand, if gay teens pretend to be something that they are not, the burden that they carry can be overwhelming. To avoid being discovered, gay teens often shy away from making friends. It's no wonder, then, that as many as 95 percent of gay teens reported feeling isolated and lonely. This often results in depression and self-hatred.[15]

Sometimes gays mask their depression with risky behavior. Several studies indicate that at least one fourth of gay teenage males get into trouble. They cut classes, run away, use drugs and alcohol, and some turn to prostitution to survive.[16]

In addition, gay males are often exposed to AIDS, a disease caused by a deadly virus. It can be spread through sexual activities or through sharing needles when using intravenous drugs.

Since harassment, abuse, isolation, and the threat of AIDS are a part of a homosexual's life, it is not surprising that the suicide rate for gays is high. According to some suicidologists, homosexuals are two to three times more likely than heterosexuals in the same age brackets to kill themselves, and more than half of the gays interviewed have thought about committing suicide. Those with AIDS are sixty-six times more likely than the general population to take their own lives in order to avoid the extraordinary suffering that accompanies the disease.[17]

Not all experts accept the various studies' conclusions that the suicide rate for homosexuals is high or the idea that there is a connection between homosexuality and suicide. Opponents of the studies attack the statistics presented by interviewers, arguing that until many more gays are questioned the conclusions are meaningless. These experts also point out that many factors play a role in teenage suicide. Writer Don Feder, who believes that homosexual suicides are a fabricated crisis, said:

> In 1991, Gallup surveyed teenagers on the leading causes of suicide. Those who said they'd attempted or thought seriously about the act were asked what factors influenced them. Drug and alcohol abuse, grades, family problems and boy-girl relationships all figured prominently.
>
> Feelings of anxiety or alienation due to homosexual tendencies didn't even register in the survey.[18]

Clearly the debate over the relationship of homosexuality and suicide is not over.

Wishful Thinking

And finally, suicide can be the result of wishful thinking. People who engage in this thinking kill themselves for very different reasons. Some may be trying to punish those who they feel have treated them badly. It is the "You'll really be sorry!" belief. Often these people arrange their deaths so that those who are to be punished will be the ones to find the body. These suicidal people may also use the gun of the person they want to punish, or they may arrange their deaths so that those targeted to be punished actually witness the suicide. For example, a middle-aged businessman who believed that his wife had somehow ruined his life called her on the telephone from his office and told her that he was going to commit suicide. After he berated her, and while she was still listening, he shot himself to death.

Revenge is not the only motive for wishful-thinking suicides. Sometimes those who commit suicide have witnessed an outpouring of grief and compliments at a funeral. Experiencing serious problems and feeling worthless, some people may try to kill themselves so that they, too, may have a similar show of love and concern.

Celebrities make headlines when they die, especially if they kill themselves. Kurt Cobain, for example, received international attention when he died. Those who think of such celebrities as heroes may also decide to kill themselves. They do so to imitate the stars, to join them in the hereafter, and to gain publicity through their deaths that they couldn't achieve by living. They may believe that they will make history, but in reality, their behavior is simply another example of wishful thinking, for the publicity, just as the revenge or the outpouring of compliments, is short-lived at best. More important, the deceased will not be present to savor the moment.

Wishful thinking may also play a part in

accidental suicides, deaths that were meant to be near misses. These suicides are usually caused by one of two things: Either the deceased wanted to draw attention to his anguish through an attempted suicide or he wanted to manipulate someone, to force him or her to do something. For instance, the deceased may have been trying to force someone to marry him by threatening suicide. Unfortunately, such schemes can backfire, and what was to be a near miss ends up becoming a completed suicide. How many of the thirty thousand annual suicides that weren't supposed to end in death is not clear. What is clear is the fact that the causes of suicide are complex. To believe otherwise is yet another form of wishful thinking.

5

How?

Although suicide is sometimes an impulsive act, the majority of would-be suicides select the method, the time, and the place of their death well in advance. A few go much further, selecting special clothing for the event, writing a lengthy farewell note, and giving away their belongings. Planning their death is especially important to those who have long felt helpless; it gives them a sense of control over their lives.

Methods Used

Suicidologists have identified at least forty different means that people use to kill themselves. The method that they select usually depends upon what is available but also varies according to gender.

According to the National Center for Health Statistics (NCHS), the majority of those who commit suicide do so by shooting themselves. In fact, the latest statistics available from the NCHS show that 59 percent of all suicides were committed with some kind of firearm. Firearms can be found in more than half of all American households.[1] Males are more likely than females to use this method, because females, who are often more concerned with appearance, even in death, may favor less disfiguring means. However, the use of firearms is growing among females, especially among teenage girls. Killing oneself with a gun is also on the rise among all teens ages fifteen to nineteen.[2] Currently, the number of suicides committed by guns in this age bracket is 66 percent.[3]

The second most common method of killing oneself is by suffocation. This includes hanging and strangulation, and it accounts for about 20 percent of all suicides. Here again, items needed to kill oneself this way—rope, for example—are available in most households.

Ingestion—taking poison or an overdose of pills— is the third most common method, used by approximately 10 percent of those wishing to end their own lives. Pills are used most often by females to avoid disfigurement and by physicians who have ready access to lethal doses. Drugs are also favored by the elderly who are taking medications, some of which could be potentially deadly in large amounts or when used in combination with alcohol.

But overdoses are not always fatal. Drugs take time to work, so if the would-be suicides are discovered in time or if they change their minds, their lives can often be saved. Because many females resort to overdoses to try to end their lives whereas males use a much faster and more deadly means—guns— explains, in part, why females are more likely than males to survive suicide attempts.

Other methods of dying, which account for about 10 percent of all suicides (the numbers vary somewhat from year to year), include leaping from a great height, slashing wrists, diving into a river to drown, or crashing automobiles. One of the most bizarre auto suicides to date was staged by a man in Wisconsin. He deliberately crashed his car into a large tank of propane gas. When flames shot out from the tank and set his car on fire, the man crawled out of his auto and into the trunk of his car, closing the lid so that escape would be impossible.

Place

The place chosen by suicidal people often has a special meaning. A middle-aged single woman who had long wanted to marry and have a family killed herself in her hope chest, a chest that once contained linens she had embroidered for her much-longed-for home. A grief-stricken widower killed himself beside his deceased wife's grave. A seriously ill opera fan killed himself by jumping from the top balcony in the

Metropolitan Opera House. One young man, whose family had moved often during his short lifetime, hanged himself on a large oak tree behind his home. This young man, according to his suicide note, was distraught over yet another move to another city. He chose the tree because it had deep roots, something he believed that his family lacked.

Sometimes a would-be suicide chooses a place known for suicide attempts, a site such as the Golden Gate Bridge in California. Since 1937, when the first person jumped to his death from the bridge, more than eight hundred people have killed themselves there, despite local authorities' attempts to prevent more deaths. To some people, the bridge, with its beautiful surroundings, is a suicide shrine.

Time

Popular myths about suicide include the false belief that suicidal people kill themselves in the middle of the night during the winter holidays, when everyone else appears to be happy and content. In reality, most suicides are committed in broad daylight in the month of May. Suicidologists believe that the sense of renewal and rebirth associated with spring and so evident in May is sometimes traumatic for suicidal people. They see new life all about them, and yet feel that there is no opportunity for them to participate. The resulting pain is more than they can stand, so they kill themselves.[4]

During other months, suicidal people who plan their deaths long in advance may choose a date that has a special significance to them. One man killed himself on July 4, Independence Day, to symbolize his freedom from anguish and pain. A mentally disturbed woman who was deeply depressed over her daughter's upcoming wedding killed herself on the day of the wedding in the church where the vows were going to be exchanged. Others committed suicide on their birthdays.

Many suicides, especially among teens, are set to take place when family members are in the house. Spouses have been known to take a handful of pills shortly before their partners were expected to return home. Experts believe that these planned suicides are not suicides at all but rather dramatic calls for help.

Clothing for the Occasion

Before the members of Heaven's Gate killed themselves, they put on special clothing, including black tennis shoes. Since all wore the same kind of clothing and were covered with unusual diamond-shaped purple shrouds, it is quite likely that these items had special meanings. Purple, for example, is used by various faiths as a symbol of spirituality. Others who have killed themselves have sometimes donned their best clothing, assuming that they would be buried in it. A few chose a garment that reminded them of a certain event or person. In the romantic story about Werther, for example, the hero died wearing a jacket that his beloved had touched and admired.

People who are imitating the death of a star not

only use the same kind of weapon that the celebrity used, but also wear clothing that represents the star. When several girls killed themselves after singer Kurt Cobain took his life, they wore T-shirts with his name and likeness.

Suicide on the Installment Plan

Because suicide still has a stigma attached to it, people who have what suicidologists call a "death wish" may try to kill themselves slowly, on what is sometimes referred to as the installment plan, or shadow suicide.

Like those who want to kill themselves outright, those who use the installment-plan method can do so in a variety of ways. Some might become heavy drinkers, consuming large quantities of alcohol until they destroy their livers. Others might smoke cigarettes until they develop lung cancer, a deadly disease, or they might take drugs. Others might eat too much, gaining far too much weight, putting strain on their hearts and clogging their arteries with fat. On the other hand, some might eat too little, depriving their bodies of much-needed nutrients. Some may drive recklessly and take chances that others would call crazy.[5]

Not all experts believe in shadow suicides. They point out that it is not unusual for depressed and distressed people to seek solace—and not necessarily death—in alcohol, cigarettes, and food. Eating too little, they add, especially among young women, simply reflects our society's obsession with being thin. And driving too fast may be nothing more than carelessness. These experts also point out that sometimes depressed people remark that instead of experiencing intense emotional pain, they feel numb. Some of these patients deliberately seek out dangerous situations just to see whether they can once again feel something, even if it's incredible fear. Suicidologists, however, agree that abusing alcohol and drugs or driving too fast are self-destructive acts that may lead to death, intentional or not.

A diet high in salt, fat, sugar, and caffeine is unhealthy, and it may contribute to what suicidologists call suicide on the installment plan. Drinking and smoking can, too.

Leaving a Note

Even though suicidal people always leave notes in the movies, in real life only one out of every five people who commits suicide leaves a message. One letter is the common number. One third of those who do write notes write several. The Wisconsinite who died in the trunk of his car, for example, tossed letters from his car window as he drove from his home toward the propane tank.

The content of suicide notes varies greatly. Because the people writing them are under great stress, it is not always possible to know whether they really meant what they said. In general, though, most of the deceased try to explain why they want to die. They may insist that no one else is responsible for their act, or they may list all whom they blame, giving numerous examples of mistreatment over the years. The following note was left by a sixteen-year-old boy named Jay. It is a good example of a message that tries to explain why someone wants to die. It also is a good example of the thoughts of a deeply depressed person. Jay said:

> Dear World,
>   I don't want to get my hair cut. I don't want to tend kids or see Tina at school on Monday. I don't want to do my biology assignment or English or history or anything. I don't want to be sad or lonely or depressed anymore. I don't want to talk, sleep, move, feel, live or breathe anymore. Tina, it's not your fault. Mom and Dad, it's not your fault. I'm not free. I feel ill. I'm sad. I'm lonely.[6]

Some choose their words to hurt as much as

possible. One young man who hanged himself next to the family Christmas tree had pinned a note to his clothing before he took his life. The note simply said: "Merry Christmas."[7]

A few suicide notes list the deceased's belongings and explain how they should be distributed. In some cases, the deceased may mail their notes along with some prized belongings, such as books or records, only hours before they take their lives. On a rare occasion, the would-be suicide may even select gifts—for an upcoming birthday, for example—before he or she dies.

Looking for More Answers

Once suicidologists had identified who committed suicide, why they did so, and how they did it, they were ready to tackle the most difficult question of all: How could they prevent suicide?

6

To Save a Life

Until the twentieth century, fear was the major weapon used to keep people from trying to commit suicide. As discussed in Chapter 2, religious leaders warned followers that all who took their own lives faced an eternity in hell. Those who tried to kill themselves but failed in their attempt were threatened with legal prosecution and scorn and contempt from their neighbors.

In addition, beginning in the 1800s, prevention often included confining attempters to mental institutions. Even though, on the average only 15 percent of suicidal people are legally insane (unable to make rational decisions), many doctors believed then that all suicidal people were mad. Why else, physicians wondered, would people try to kill themselves? The first institutions were little more than warehouses for mentally ill people. The most dangerous patients were restrained in straitjackets, and more than a few of these screamed and shouted for hours on end. The scene before them made some attempters more suicidal than ever.

Prevention With a Heart

Finally, in the early 1900s, a few brave souls began to think of suicide as a worthy area of study. They saw suicidal people as human beings, not hell-bound sinners who were crazy to boot. Social workers and counselors began to develop programs to prevent suicide attempts and to help attempters who survived. Most important of all, counselors did not resort to using scare tactics—which had failed for hundreds of years—to try to keep people from killing themselves.

The Save-A-Life League

One of the first professionals to work in the prevention field was Harry Marsh Warren, a Baptist minister. In 1906 he started the Save-A-Life League in New York City. As a minister, Warren had been asked to counsel people who had tried to kill themselves. He quickly realized that many attempters had mixed feelings; they wanted to live, but they saw no way to end their unbearable misery other than death. Warren also discovered that many suicidal people just needed someone to talk to or a little help to get them through a temporary, but overwhelming, crisis. Believing that many suicides could be prevented, he openly sought suicidal people for counseling. Eventually the league had representatives in thirty-five cities across the nation, and it claimed to have saved at least one thousand lives each year.

Even though Warren's league was successful for more than forty years, his counselors remained among the few who tried to prevent suicide. Psychiatrists and psychologists shied away from suicidal patients for two reasons. First, most believed that they were ill-equipped to handle suicidal people, because there were no guidelines and few studies available to help them determine how best to treat such patients. Second, therapists feared failure, knowing that it could result in the loss of lives.

The Los Angeles Suicide Prevention Center

Then, in 1949, Edwin Shneidman and Norman L. Farberow, two psychologists, began a scientific study of the prevention of suicide. They analyzed suicide notes, more than seven hundred in all, and talked at length to survivors and those who had attempted to take their own lives. What, they kept asking attempters, would have prevented you from trying to kill yourself?

After years of study and armed with many suggestions, they opened a suicide prevention center in Los Angeles, California, in 1958. They were joined by Robert E. Litman, a director of a psychiatric unit in a nearby hospital.

With no model to follow, the counselors at the Los Angeles Suicide Prevention Center had to make their own rules as they went along. They set up a hot line and asked for referrals from local psychiatrists and psychologists, who were greatly relieved to have someone to whom they could refer their suicidal patients. Then Shneidman and Farberow advertised their services to the community. They were quickly flooded with calls.

After working with a number of would-be suicide committers, prevention counselors developed a good sense of who was at great risk and needed to be hospitalized or watched around the clock until their crisis could be resolved. Eventually, the counselors developed tests that could identify these high-risk individuals.

Although the center's counselors did a lot of listening and gave out plenty of advice, they were not above doing the unthinkable in the counseling world if it would result in saving a life. For example, on one occasion, they threw a suicidal woman into a counselor's car, and they ordered her brother to sit on her until they reached the hospital.[1]

The center was successful, and as more and more people sought its services, including people from other cities, more communities decided to open similar facilities. Today, there are crisis centers and hot lines all over the country. They are listed in the Yellow Pages of telephone books, and most are operated twenty-four hours a day. Counselors, thanks to intensive training, are well-equipped to handle questions and concerns regarding all types of crises, including suicide. Hot-line callers can remain anonymous if they so choose, and they may call as often as they need.

Counselors take their crisis center jobs very seriously. As one said:

> There's no special magic that will give a caller a new life or that will keep a caller from committing suicide if he really wants to. All you can do is listen, really listen. That's what people need when they're hurting. You may think that listening's not very much, but you may be the first person to ever listen to them. And you may be the last.[2]

Other Sources of Help

In addition to counselors in crisis centers, suicidal people today can receive help from school counselors, clergy, family physicians, and professional therapists who specialize in suicide prevention. Besides providing guidance, these professionals can put those thinking about suicide and actual attempters in touch with support groups. If drug or alcohol abuse is also a problem, counselors can make referrals to such groups as Alcoholics Anonymous and Narcotics Anonymous for additional help.

Getting Help

Ideally, suicidal people should seek help on their own. Unfortunately, they seldom do. They may believe that having problems means that they've somehow done something wrong and, therefore, they deserve to be punished. Also, because they may have been deeply disappointed by others, suicidal people may be afraid to trust others or to reach out for help. Why ask for help, they might reason, when they aren't likely to receive it? Besides, no one, they might think, could possibly understand their pain or resolve their irresolvable problems.

When would-be suicide attempters are children, they have an additional concern. They feel guilty about even thinking of going to someone other than their parents for help. They believe that talking about their problems with strangers would betray their family and anger their parents. This is especially true if children have been ordered to keep certain events in their home a secret.

Identifying Those at Risk

If suicidal people won't seek advice, the most logical people to find help for them would be friends and relatives. Many try to do so. Sometimes, though, suicidal people have become socially isolated. They have few friends, and their families may be one of the reasons that the would-be suicides want to die. In such cases, these people are at the mercy of teachers, classmates, coworkers, or neighbors, anyone who might notice their distress and reach out to them.

Since all suicidal people do not behave in the same manner, the warning signs of an impending suicide vary from person to person. Even so, there are some common behaviors. In addition to being deeply depressed for some time (see Chapter 4 for a description of depressed people) and having a serious drug or alcohol problem, suicidal people may have experienced a traumatic event recently—serious trouble in school, for example—that has sent them reeling. (See the chart on Triggering Events below for examples of more traumatic events.) They may also be obsessed with death and dying, and they may have talked about committing suicide. In addition, if the person has made the decision to die, the would-be suicide attempter, after months of feeling despondent and hopeless, may suddenly seem at peace.

Triggering Events

Very stressful events can lead to depression or serve as a triggering event for suicide in an already deeply depressed person. Such events include

- The death of a loved one or a hero especially if the death was due to suicide
- The loss of a valued position—a good job, for instance
- Serious trouble in school, failure or expulsion
- Difficulty with the law
- Public humiliation by peers or family members
- Failure to achieve a goal, particularly by individuals who tend to be perfectionists
- The onset of a painful, incurable illness
- An unplanned pregnancy
- The breakup of a romance
- Disruption in the home, a divorce, a remarriage, a move to another city, serious conflicts among family members

---

Taking Action

If you think that someone you know is suicidal, it is important to take immediate action to try to save his or her life. Experts on suicide suggest that you begin by talking to the potential suicide attempter, listening to every word and watching facial expressions for clues. Repeat, in your own words, what you are told, making sure that you understand what is being said. For example, if the person says that he feels that his future is full of nothing but problems and then cites reasons for feeling this way, don't argue with him or deny his feelings. Saying "You think that your future holds nothing but problems" will at least make him aware that you heard what he said.

Ask him whether he is thinking about committing suicide. Don't hint or try to be subtle. Just say, "Are you thinking about killing yourself?" If he is thinking about dying, ask about a plan. The more detailed the plan, the more likely it is that this person is at high risk to try to end his life. If he has begun to act on his plan, giving away belongings, for example, or saying good-bye to classmates, his life is at great risk. Have someone stay with him until you can get help.

Even if a plan doesn't exist, seek help from an adult or a professional counselor at the earliest possible moment. Do not try to solve the problem yourself, believing that you have the skills to do so. Suicidal people are difficult to predict and more difficult to treat. Even professionals who deal with such patients every day are not always successful. This is not the time to take a chance.

Also, this is not the time to keep secrets. Betraying a confidence is difficult for anyone, especially teens, since they are intensely loyal to peers. Even if you have promised not to repeat what was said, remember that a life is at stake. Seek help from a trusted adult or call a crisis hot line.

Treatment

Whether would-be suicide attempters are thinking about killing themselves or have already attempted to do so—there are one hundred thousand failed suicide attempts each year—the recommended treatment depends on the risk. Attempters and people at high-risk for suicide may be hospitalized for a while. They are usually given medications such as tranquilizers—which have been in use since 1954—to calm them, or antidepressants to temporarily ease their emotional pain. The medications will not solve the suicidal person's problems, nor will they remove the risk of suicide, unless a chemical imbalance—and only a chemical imbalance—is to blame. In most cases, medications simply make the high-risk individual more receptive to counseling.

Hospitalization provides several advantages. It gives suicidal people—and their loved ones—security, and it provides high-risk individuals with a quiet atmosphere in which to think about the crises that made them want to die. Also, unlike mental hospitals in the past, suicidal people now receive intensive counseling that can help them begin to resolve their problems.

On the other hand, hospitalization is not available to everyone. It can be very expensive, more than one thousand dollars a day in a private institution. Not all health insurance plans pay for confining suicidal patients, nor can all suicidal people or their families foot the bills. In addition, some states make it very difficult to hospitalize a patient against his or her will for more than several days, and some suicidal patients are not willing to be institutionalized.

Counseling for suicidal patients, in or outside of the hospital, tries to help them resolve their problems and find a reason to live. Often would-be suicide attempters have put most of their energy into a job or relationship. If they lose their position or their friend, they have nothing to fall back on until they can replace the loss. Counselors help suicidal people realize that they need to have more than one important thing in their lives, and they help them take steps to make that happen.

Patients are also encouraged to join a support group, for which fees, if they exist, are very low. At meetings, members—all of whom are or were suicidal—can share their feelings with others without the fear of being judged or ridiculed. Also, as members make progress, they serve as role models for incoming would-be suicides, giving members respect, status, and a reason to live.

Unfortunately, even though many resources are available, not all at high risk for suicide and attempters will receive the counseling that they need. Some, as already mentioned, believe that everything is hopeless, and they will refuse all offers of help.

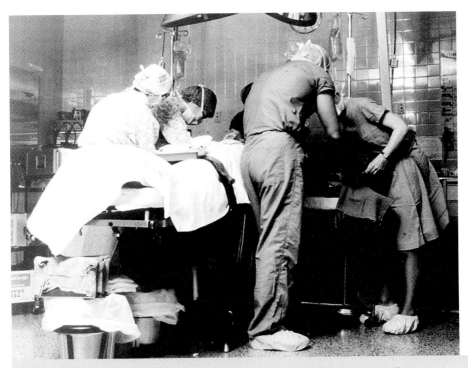

Suicide attempters may need emergency treatment to save their lives. If physical damage is not too great, attempters may go on to lead normal lives with the help of intensive counseling.

Others, like a teenager named Charles, will be denied help. Charles tried to hang himself. His parents did not take his attempt seriously, and when they brought him home from the hospital, they refused to contact the counselors and the suicide support group that the doctors at the hospital had recommended. Charles's mother insisted that the attempted hanging was just a silly misunderstanding. For a while Charles, who was very good at masking his depression, seemed happier than before. He even joked about the rope marks on his neck. A few months later, he hanged himself again, and this time he successfully completed his suicide attempt.[3]

Charles's parents weren't the only ones to deny their child's problem. Study after study shows that parents believe that the thought of suicide has never crossed their children's minds. And even after an attempt is made, as many as 41 percent of parents who are told to get help fail to do so.[4]

Special Precautions

On March 11, 1987, four teenagers in Bergenfield, New Jersey—Cheryl Burress, seventeen; Lisa Burress, her sixteen-year-old sister; Thomas Olton, eighteen; and Thomas Rizzo, nineteen—decided to kill themselves. They drove to a vacant garage, closed the door, rolled down the windows in their car, and left the car's engine running. While they waited for the garage to fill up with carbon monoxide, a deadly gas, they wrote suicide notes.

Like other unusual suicide cases, these made the evening news all across the country. Although the teens were not the first to commit multiple suicide, they made popular the phrase "cluster suicides." But as reporters and investigators began to piece together the events that led to the four deaths, these suicides except for the number were not unusual. Like many other suicides, all four of the deceased had become overwhelmed by personal problems. Both boys had serious drug problems, and the girls were struggling—unsuccessfully—with their mother's remarriage. In addition, all four showed signs of masked depression, and they had been acting out in school. Three had finally dropped out, and Lisa had recently been suspended.

Also, all four mourned the death of a close friend, Joe Major, who had died under mysterious circumstances a few months before. Major's death had been ruled an accident, but most of his friends thought that his fall from a cliff, several hundred feet high, was a suicide. Three of the four who died had been with Major when he went over the edge.

Two days after the four teens in New Jersey died, two teens in Alsip, Illinois—Nancy Grannan, nineteen, and Karen Logan, seventeen—killed themselves. They, too, died in a carbon-monoxide-filled garage. And like the New Jersey teens, they had become overwhelmed by personal problems. These teens had dropped out of school, and neither could find a job. In addition, both had been drinking heavily for several days before they killed themselves. Grannan and Logan had probably been considering suicide for some time, but it wasn't until the news about the cluster suicides in New Jersey reached them—a triggering event—that they decided to take their lives in exactly the same manner. Their deaths were copycat suicides.

Copycat suicides are usually committed by deeply upset teenagers. As a result, school counselors usually play a key role in prevention. Now, as soon as a teen suicide takes place in a community, counselors hold large group sessions in school to discuss the event, help students deal with their grief, and try to assess the risk for more deaths in the school and the community itself. (Similar sessions may also be held in schools all across the nation if the first death received a lot of attention.) It may seem like a lot of effort to talk to thousands of students to ward off potential suicides, but counselors consider saving even one life worth all of the hard work.

Myths About Suicide

Below are some of the most commonly believed myths concerning suicide.

Myth: People who talk about committing suicide never actually go through with it. They just want attention.

Fact: People who talk about killing themselves must be taken seriously. It may be a cry for attention, but it is much more likely that these people plan to do away with themselves unless someone intervenes.

Myth: People who survive a suicide attempt never try again.

Fact: About 80 percent of suicides have made at least one previous attempt.

Myth: You should never mention the word *suicide* to depressed people. It might give them the idea to do away with themselves.

Fact: Most depressed people have already thought about killing themselves. Talking to them about dying gives you an opportunity to determine whether the person is likely to commit suicide, and if so, to get help.

Myth: People who are receiving counseling never commit suicide.

Fact: It takes a long time to help suicidal people, the majority of whom are deeply depressed, find a reason to live. Sometimes progress is so slow that they give up and kill themselves.

Myth: People from "good" families never commit suicide.

Fact: Wealth, education, and social status do not protect families from suicide. It is found in all economic and social classes in America.

Myth: People who have attempted suicide remain suicidal for the rest of their life.

Fact: Many, but not all, suicidal people go on to lead happy, productive lives if they can find a reason to live. Since this is nearly impossible for suicidal people to do on their own, counseling is a must.

7

The Right to Die

Until recently, serious health problems often resulted in death. But now, hospitals have the equipment to keep us alive indefinitely. If we can't breathe, artificial respirators can do it for us. When we can't drink or eat, intravenous tubes will provide us with much-needed liquids and nutrients. If our hearts are worn out, pumps can circulate our blood until donor hearts can be found.

These health aids, and many more, were meant to keep patients alive until they were able to breathe, drink, eat, and pump blood on their own. In some cases, though, there is little hope for any recovery, and patients who face years of being connected to machines with nothing to look forward to have questioned why they should continue to live. Others have argued, as did St. Augustine more than fifteen hundred years ago, that life is a gift from God and every effort should be made to maintain it. The result was a heated debate about the right to die that eventually led to an even more heated debate about the right to assisted suicide.

The Right-to-Die Issue

In 1975, twenty-one-year-old Karen Ann Quinlan took a handful of tranquilizers followed by several alcoholic drinks. Shortly after, she fell into a coma and was rushed to a nearby hospital. Her breathing was irregular, so doctors placed her on a respirator. When she did not regain consciousness, she was placed on a feeding tube as well.

As soon as tests were completed, the Quinlans were told that Karen had suffered so much brain damage that there was no hope for even a partial recovery. Instead, she could remain in a coma for years before dying.

After weeks of agonizing discussions with specialists, the Quinlans finally asked the doctors to take Karen off the respirator so that she might die. Today, withdrawing or withholding medical treatment when there is no hope of recovery is not uncommon. However, in 1975 when doctors were expected to keep a patient alive at all costs, it was a shocking request. Karen's physicians were afraid of being accused of malpractice, even murder, and they absolutely refused to honor the Quinlans' appeal.

When the Quinlans couldn't get help from the medical profession, they made an appeal in a New Jersey courtroom—the first of its kind. They wanted the court to order the doctors to remove Karen from the respirator. Their lawyer argued that keeping Karen alive was unconstitutional because it was nothing less than cruel and unusual punishment. On the other hand, an attorney for the state, who was assigned to protect Karen's interests, argued that removing her from the respirator would be a crime. Allowing her to die, he said, was murder, pure and simple.

Karen's doctors were also represented in court. Their lawyer argued that no one knew beyond a shadow of a doubt that Karen would never recover. Why not, they asked, give her every opportunity to at least regain consciousness? Besides, doctors had taken an oath to preserve life, not to take it away. If her doctors allowed her to die, the lawyer wondered, wouldn't all Americans become leery of the medical profession? And wouldn't that forever damage the relationship between patients and their physicians?

The Quinlans lost the first round in court, but upon appeal, they were given the right that they sought. In a landmark decision in 1976, the State Supreme Court in New Jersey ordered the doctors to remove Karen Ann Quinlan from the respirator, and only the respirator, which they did shortly after. Instead of dying, though, Karen, barely breathing on her own at times, lived another nine years. During this time, her weight dropped from 120 pounds to 60 pounds, and she remained in a coma to the very end.

The Quinlan case was just the beginning in a long series of legal battles for the right to die that spanned fifteen years. Finally, in 1990, the most influential case of all reached the United States Supreme Court. This case involved Nancy Cruzan, who was in a coma and had irreversible brain damage. The Supreme Court decided that her parents had the right to have Nancy's feeding tubes removed so that she could die. The justices stated that there was no justifiable reason to prolong a life against overwhelming odds. This set a national precedent.

By this time, the public, thanks to the media, was very familiar with the right-to-die issue and the heart-wrenching cases behind it. As each case made the headlines, a few more people decided to join the cause. By the time the Cruzan case was decided, 70 percent of all Americans supported the right to die. This was a dramatic change in viewpoint, for just twenty-five years earlier, only 35 percent believed that a patient, or his or her representative, should have the right to refuse treatment.

Today, some Americans continue to debate the right-to-die issue. However, one woman recently spoke for many when she said:

> Too many people treat death like it must be avoided at all costs. Physicians feel a patient's death is their personal failure. Families feel they must ask that everything be done to keep loved

ones alive. Often, this results in a beating heart and lungs that are maintained by machines. This is not life.[1]

Assisted Suicide

Once the majority of people accepted withholding treatment from patients who had no hope of recovery, the public turned its attention to an even more controversial issue: assisted suicide. What if, Americans asked, terminally ill patients were in unbearable pain, wanted to die, but were unable to commit suicide by themselves? What if withdrawing medical treatment to *let* them die would not result in immediate death? Should someone *help* them end their life?

Dr. Kevorkian Takes Center Stage

While the public debated assisted suicide, Dr. Jack Kevorkian took action. In 1990, the same year that the United States Supreme Court ruled in the Cruzan case, Kevorkian helped Janet Adkins, a fifty-four-year-old woman from Oregon who suffered from Alzheimer's disease, commit suicide.

Adkins and her husband traveled to Michigan, where Kevorkian lived, to receive the doctor's aid. When they met, Kevorkian asked Adkins a few questions, decided that she was able to make decisions for herself, and discussed how she would die. In this case, Kevorkian favored death by asphyxiation, and he explained how it was to be done.

On June 4, 1990, Adkins climbed into the back of Kevorkian's van in a state park, lay down on a cot, and waited for the carbon monoxide flowing into the van from a hose connected to the exhaust pipe to kill her. Kevorkian turned her body over to authorities for an autopsy before announcing her death to a stunned public.

Kevorkian then set out to find others whose suicides he could assist. Newspaper ads were one means of finding more patients. One ad read: "Oppressed by a fatal disease, a severe handicap, a crippling deformity? . . . Show him proper compelling medical evidence that you should die, and Dr. Jack Kevorkian will help you kill yourself, free of charge."[2]

In addition to the carbon monoxide hookup, Kevorkian invented a suicide machine that patients could use. This device consisted of a stand with long plastic tubes and needles connected to three separate containers, each filled with a different liquid: a saline solution to enable the other fluids to enter the bloodstream more easily; a sedative to calm the suicidal person; and potassium chloride, a poison, to end the person's life. When the needles were inserted into a vein and a lever was pressed, death followed shortly after.

During the next eight years, Kevorkian claimed to have helped at least one hundred people kill themselves. Some Americans regarded him as an angel of mercy. Others, horrified by the mounting numbers, began to call him Dr. Death, and worse. Legal authorities in Michigan, where all of the deaths took place, called him a murderer. They wondered aloud how

Dr. Jack Kevorkian, who invented a suicide machine, supports assisted suicide.

some of his applicants who were paralyzed could have operated the suicide machine by themselves or climbed into the back of his van.

Prosecutors also questioned the standards that Kevorkian used for accepting patients. Autopsy reports indicated that some of the deceased did not have serious health problems. For example, reports showed that Kevorkian's thirty-third patient, Rebecca Badger, who insisted that she had an advanced case of multiple sclerosis, was not seriously ill. Instead, when medical authorities questioned the doctor who diagnosed Badger's illness, he admitted that he had been deceived by her. After her death, he had learned that Badger had a long history of drug addiction. She also possessed the medical knowledge needed to convince doctors that she was sick and in need of the painkillers to which she was addicted.[3]

Besides questioning Kevorkian's standards for acceptance, prosecutors questioned his methods as well. When rumors surfaced that one of his patients tried to change his mind at the last minute but was not allowed to do so, authorities took an even closer look at the doctor's activities. Eventually they decided that they had enough evidence to arrest and try him.

To date, Kevorkian has been tried five times. At the first four trials, relatives of the deceased testified that their loved one was in agony and wanted to die but was unable to so without help. Either he or she lacked the means to commit suicide or the confidence that such an attempt would be fatal.

In March 1999, Kevorkian was convicted of

second-degree murder in the injection death of 52-year-old Thomas Youk. He was also convicted of delivery of a controlled substance, used to make the lethal injection. Youk was suffering from amyotrophic lateral sclerosis (also called Lou Gehrig's disease), an ultimately fatal disease of the spinal cord. Though Youk had requested Kevorkian's assistance, prosecutors in the state of Michigan were allowed to try Kevorkian for murder. Kevorkian unsuccessfully defended himself.

Youk's family was not allowed to testify because the judge ruled that their testimony was irrelevant to the murder. If Kevorkian had been tried for assisted suicide, as in the first four cases, relatives could have testified.

At the time this book went to press, Kevorkian was sentenced to ten to twenty-five years in prison.

Kevorkian had long talked about performing experiments on the dying and harvesting organs—hearts, livers, lungs, and kidneys—from his patients. On June 7, 1998, Kevorkian began the second phase of his assisted-suicide program: He supervised the removal of kidneys from Joseph Tushkowski, a quadriplegic who had been paralyzed for twenty-one years. After dropping Tushkowski's corpse off at a local hospital, Kevorkian announced that he had two kidneys to donate. And he indicated that there would be more to come in the future. He said, "Just as Janet Adkins was the first, this is the first of the line."[4]

However, even though many donors await organs, it is highly unlikely that any that Kevorkian offers will be accepted even when he is released. Organs must be taken under highly regulated conditions and many tests must be performed to guarantee that the organs are disease-free and are a perfect match for a waiting donor. Most doctors doubt that Kevorkian's secret site and testing methods would meet the necessary standards. Besides, because he lost his doctor's license years ago, hospitals refuse to work with Kevorkian. It is unlikely that hospitals will reconsider.

The Hemlock Society

While Dr. Kevorkian's assisted suicides grabbed headlines, a group known as the Hemlock Society worked quietly behind the scenes to help the terminally ill kill themselves. This organization was started by Derek Humphry in 1980, and it was named after the poison given to Greek citizens to end their lives. The society has promoted its cause primarily through a newsletter called the *Hemlock Quarterly*. This publication talked about suicide in general, accepted letters from subscribers who argued for assisted suicide for terminally ill patients, and printed testimonials of those who had helped a loved one die.

In 1988 the society decided to stop talking about suicide and tell subscribers exactly how to do it. One of the *Quarterly* issues contained a list of drugs that could kill that if taken in large enough doses. It then listed the deadly amount needed. Because almost all of the drugs listed were regulated medications and required a prescription from a doctor, the newsletter gave tips on how to obtain the medicines, including faking an illness and smuggling drugs from abroad.

The society also began to offer legal advice if subscribers were arrested for helping someone die. From the beginning, the society was not only successful in winning cases in court, but was also able to gain more and more supporters. By the mid-1990s, the Hemlock Society had almost forty thousand members. As the demand for information about suicide continued to grow, Derek Humphry wrote *Final Exit*, his now famous book about how to commit suicide. It was so detailed that Humphry believed that anyone who followed the directions could commit suicide or aid in an attempt. This book became a bestseller in 1991.

Assisted Suicide in Oregon

The demand for Dr. Kevorkian's help and the success of the Hemlock Society and Humphry's book caused quite a stir everywhere and led to a debate about legalizing assisted suicide. The results were very different in different states. While Michigan legislators tried to write a law that would stop Kevorkian, citizens in California, Washington, and Oregon voted on laws that would permit physician-assisted suicide. Voters in California and Washington rejected the idea, but in Oregon in 1994 the electorate passed Initiative 119, which paved the way for the first law in America that made physician-assisted suicide legal. This law, the

Death with Dignity Act (DDA), received only 51 percent of the votes, and it was—and still is—very controversial.

Once the people had passed the initiative, legislators set out to write a law that would do three things. First and foremost, it would help patients with less than six months to live end their lives when they wished to do so. Second, it would make these suicides as easy and as painless as possible. Third, it would make sure that the DDA had very specific limits to prevent abuses.

To achieve these goals, legislators included a number of safeguards to protect patients. Applicants must make a written request for help. They will then be interviewed by two doctors, who will look for signs of depression and examine the applicants' medical records. The doctors will also explore the possibility that applicants are being pressured to die because of mounting medical bills or exhausted caregivers. If the doctors believe that the applicants are acting only out of depression or are unable to make an informed decision or do not really want to die, assistance will be denied. If assistance is offered, applicants must then undergo a waiting period of fifteen days—time to really think about their decision.

At the end of the waiting period, a physician will write a prescription for a lethal dose of medication and give specific instructions on how to take it. This ensures as quick and as painless a death as possible. To make sure that an applicant has every opportunity to change his or her mind and that the act is suicide, not murder, the patient must take the pills; no one else may administer them.

To safeguard the state, participants are regulated. Only residents of Oregon may request assistance. This eliminates the possibility of turning Oregon into a suicide mecca. Also, doctors who choose to participate in the program must be licensed in Oregon and follow the state's rules. Records have to be available for examination at any time.

As soon as the law was passed, opponents appealed to the courts to strike it down. Meanwhile the act remained on the books but could not be used.

Opponents, led primarily by church groups and right-to-life (antiabortion) leaders, believed that assisted suicide was morally wrong. They referred to long-held beliefs by religious leaders: Suicide, assisted or self-inflicted, was nothing less than murder; suicide was a rejection of God's gift of life and, therefore, God; and finally, suicide was the act of a mere mortal who was trying to make decisions that only God should make.

Some opponents also believed that assisted suicide could lead to early deaths for defenseless victims. These opponents asked many questions. How many of those who would inherit the family fortune might speed up the dying process a bit through assisted suicide? How many elderly who were undergoing expensive medical treatment might choose to end their lives early in order to protect their families from skyrocketing expenses and a prolonged emotional ordeal? Would the *right* to choose death, opponents wondered, become a *duty* to die?

In addition, more than a few opponents worried about the potential for doctors to make mistakes. Was there a possibility that someone might be told that he or she had a fatal disease and decide to die, when in reality he or she was not terminally ill?

Among the opponents to the Death with Dignity Act were many doctors. They argued, as had the doctors in the Karen Ann Quinlan case, that physicians were expected to preserve life, not take it. How could they possibly help someone end his or her life? Furthermore, doctors added, what would assisted suicide do to the trust between physician and patient, which was so necessary for good medical care?

While opponents in Oregon attacked the bill publicly, they continued to put the issue before judges, hoping one of them would strike down the act. As the case moved through the courts all the way to the United States Supreme Court, these opponents followed assisted-suicide cases in other states, especially *Glucksberg* v. *Washington State* and *Quill* v. *Vacco* (New York State), in which Drs. Harold Glucksberg and Timothy E. Quill were challenging their own states' bans on assisted suicide. They argued that Americans had a constitutional right to end unbearable suffering with a doctor's help. Both of these cases reached the Supreme Court in January 1997. On June 26, 1997, the Court issued its opinion: The justices denied a sweeping right to assisted suicide, which supporters of assisted suicide had sought, and allowed the laws banning assisted suicide to stand.[5]

At first this appeared to be good news for

Assisted suicide is a hotly debated topic. Derek Humphry argues about assisted suicide with Dr. Ira Byock, who is deeply opposed to helping anyone take his or her life.

opponents of assisted suicide in Oregon. However, on October 15, 1997, the Supreme Court refused to hear arguments concerning the DDA, dashing opponents' hopes of any court support. Chief Justice William Rehnquist announced, as he had in the Washington and New York cases, that the issue of assisted suicide should be decided in the public arena.[6] The citizens of Washington and New York had outlawed assisted suicide of any kind; the citizens of Oregon had voted to legalize a very limited procedure. So be it. The Court's refusal to hear the case made it possible for Oregon physicians to begin to provide assistance to terminally ill patients who wished to commit suicide.

Opponents refused to give up, though. They had already persuaded the state legislature to ask Oregonians to vote on the DDA again. Ballots were mailed on October 16, 1997, as previously planned, one day after the Supreme Court's decision. When citizens voted again for the act, this time by a larger margin, opponents sought other means to abolish the law. To date, all efforts have failed, including a special appeal to the United States attorney general.

So far, only ten assisted suicides, all of terminally ill patients, have taken place in Oregon. The first occurred on March 24, 1998. An unidentified woman in her mid-eighties (her family refused to release her name) who was in the advanced stages of breast cancer died thirty minutes after taking a lethal dose of barbiturates. She died in her home, surrounded by family members. In a tape made earlier that day about her upcoming death, she said, "I'm looking forward to it. . . . I've always been able to get around and do things. Suddenly I'm in a position [where] I can't walk very good and I'm having trouble breathing."[7]

Supporters of assisted suicide are now considering putting the issue to a vote in other states. Whether they will be successful is not certain. What is certain is the fact that the issue of assisted suicide will remain in the headlines for years to come.

8

Life After Death

Those who lose a loved one to suicide have an especially difficult time coming to terms with their loss. They are not only suddenly overwhelmed with grief, but also burdened with guilt and anger and shocked by the violence that accompanied the suicide.

Guilt

Although any death is painful for survivors, sudden death may be especially hurtful, because there is no opportunity to say goodbye or to resolve conflicts. For suicide survivors, these unresolved issues often take on a special meaning; survivors sometimes see the conflicts as *the* reason for the suicide, blaming themselves for their loved one's death.

This assumption is sometimes reinforced by people in the deceased's community. Because suicides are more newsworthy and create more curiosity than most deaths, they are often highlighted by the media. Therefore, it is not unusual for strangers to point to survivors or even to question the mourners. Sometimes the questions are cruel. One mother was actually asked—repeatedly—"What did you *do* to her?"[1] after her daughter committed suicide. The result was overwhelming guilt.

Also, survivors may repeatedly review past events, looking for any clue that might have predicted the suicide. If they recall even the slightest sign that their loved one thought about dying, they berate themselves for not having reacted to it quickly enough. If they don't find a clue, they put themselves down for not being intelligent or sensitive enough to have spotted the deceased's anguish.

Anger

In addition to guilt, suicide survivors often feel anger, even rage, toward the deceased. This anger comes from a feeling of abandonment, of deliberately—and dramatically!—being left behind. Anne-Marie, a young woman whose brother killed himself, said:

> I scream, I yell out the window. . . . I have never felt this angry in my whole entire life. Angrier than I ever was at my mother or my father for not being

there. It's so frustrating! Because I always had . . . my brother. . . . I keep thinking, why did you do this to me?[2]

Left unresolved, this anger can lead to more problems. Some survivors lash out at others, accusing them of causing the deceased's death, making others feel guilty. Anne-Marie, for example, blamed her sister-in-law for her brother's death. "I have *hatred* toward my sister-in-law," she stated, "intense hatred."[3] Venting their rage at others often strains relationships to the breaking point at the very time that survivors need contact with other people. On the other hand, bottling up anger can lead to depression.

Trauma

Because suicide is violent, it sometimes traumatizes, or shocks, those who are left behind. This makes it very difficult for them to deal with their loss. They can't concentrate or sleep, and they feel helpless. Although this is not unusual for anyone who has lost a loved one, suicide survivors may have an additional emotion: fear. They constantly worry that someone else they love will kill themselves as well. Their fears are not unfounded. Survivors are eight times more likely to attempt suicide than the typical American. Counselors believe that once one family member has committed suicide, other family members see it as an acceptable way to end their agony.

While survivors are learning how to cope with their trauma, they are under so much stress that they are physically at great risk. Survivors are prone to ulcers, high blood pressure, heart attacks, and accidents. Some turn to drugs or alcohol to ease their pain, creating even more problems. Counselors estimate that it often takes suicide survivors as long as three years to come to terms with their feelings.

Because their emotional scars are many and deep, some survivors find it impossible to heal. As a result, the traumatic event haunts them for the rest of their lives. This is especially troublesome for young survivors who have many years ahead of them. One survivor said, "When I was 16, my father shot himself. I am now 77 . . . and I am still not over it."[4] Another recalled:

> My father committed suicide when I was 11. Five years later, my brother did the same—with his police revolver. He killed not only himself but his wife and their two young sons. None of this made sense to anyone who knew him. Now, 30 years later, it still doesn't make any sense. . . . The pain . . . never goes away.[5]

Lack of Support

Since a stigma is still attached to suicide, survivors seldom receive the support from their community and even friends that they might have had under different circumstances. The lack of support may hamper a survivor's ability to heal. A woman whose son killed himself said, "Losing my son was painful enough, but the whispers . . . being avoided, having people not look me in the eye, or acting like nothing happened, never mentioning the death, changing the subject . . . is almost worse."[6]

Furthermore, because a suicide is so painful, family members sometimes refuse to deal with the death. One survivor said, "Nobody in the family wants to talk about it. You have to pretend that something terrible didn't happen."[7] Often in such situations, the deceased's room is kept exactly as it was, as if he or she might return anytime. In other cases, everything belonging to the deceased is packed and stored away, as if he or she had never existed. In either case, family members are forced to deal with the loss individually. This is difficult to do, especially for children, who have the fewest skills and life experiences to handle such a traumatic event.

Young Survivors of a Parent's Death

Children who lose a parent to suicide are at great risk for serious emotional problems. First of all, this is probably their first experience with death, and they are completely unprepared to deal with so great a loss. In fact, very young children find it hard to even express their feelings at such a time. Teens, who are trying to establish their independence, do not necessarily want to talk about the event with adults. And few of their friends are likely to have had any experience with suicide, making it difficult for them to offer the support that survivors need. Also, because teens want to be like everyone else and a suicide in the family sets them apart, teenage survivors may even try to deny their grief, which can result in depression.

Second, family members, hoping to spare young children, may not tell the children the whole story. The children respond by making up their own version of what happened. In most cases, they assume that it was something that they did—or didn't do—that led to their parent's death. If they had been better children, they reason, their father or mother would not have wanted to leave them. Sometimes they believe that they are so bad that they are unloveable. They react by withdrawing from friends and relatives at the very time that they need support.

Third, if children find their parent's body, they are not only severely traumatized, but also sometimes overwhelmed by guilt, believing that they could have done something to prevent the death. One eight-year-old girl whose father had hanged himself tried to push him up into the air to loosen his noose when she found his body. Even years later, she had difficulty accepting the fact that she could not have saved his life.[8]

Fourth, all children who have lost a parent have lost an important role model and companion. Sixteen-year-old Tommy Rodgers, whose father killed himself when Tommy was ten years old, misses being able to talk to his father. He said, "I really don't have someone to talk to about guy stuff." Other relatives and friends can't take his father's place, Tommy added. "I don't really look up to them as much."[9]

Finally, the deceased will not be present for special occasions in their children's lives—graduations and weddings, for example. The fact that the parent chose to miss these events is very painful, so painful that Tommy has some advice to any parent thinking about committing suicide. "Don't do it. It will hurt all your friends and family a lot. It's not worth it. You should just try to get help."[10]

Children and the Death of a Sibling

The suicide of a brother or sister can be as painful for children as losing a parent. In addition to struggling with their grief and worrying that something they said or did caused the death, young survivors may also experience extreme jealousy when they see their parents grieving for the deceased. Mom and Dad, they reason, really did love my dead brother or sister best. Also, it is not uncommon for parents who have lost a child to become overprotective of their remaining children. Therefore, the surviving children may never learn how to become independent, self-sufficient adults.

Right-to-Die Survivors

Great sympathy has been generated over the years by highly publicized court cases that were fought by family members for the right of a terminally ill person to die, whether by pulling the plug on a respirator or withholding food or asking for drugs. Because these patients had no hope of recovery—unlike deeply depressed teenagers—many people can accept the patients' decision to die. So survivors of these deaths usually do not experience the guilt or intense anger at the deceased that overwhelms most survivors of suicide. This doesn't mean that these survivors don't experience anger, though, only this time the anger is directed at the living, not the deceased. Sometimes survivors of assisted suicide are made to feel that they must defend the deceased's decision, and on occasion, even assisted suicide in general. Jonathan Smith's fight to defend his mother's decision to die is but one example. Mrs. Smith, who was dying from fallopian cancer, an especially painful disease, eventually refused to eat in order to hasten her death in 1989. This was done with her doctor's approval. Jonathan Smith, who was

Survivors are overwhelmed with grief when a loved one dies. When that loved one has committed suicide, survivors often feel guilty and ashamed as well.

only eighteen years old at the time, was not only upset by questions he faced then, but also continues to be upset whenever someone questions an assisted suicide. Recently he wrote in an article titled "How Dare You Judge My Mom's Decision to Die":

> I get a little incensed with those who [pretend] to know better than those who are suffering as to what is right and moral. Such attitudes [belittle] the integrity, character and memory of my mother, and there is not one person on earth worthy of doing so. . . . To those who would . . . pass judgment upon others who suffer, I suggest that you get to know those who are suffering. . . . Don't you dare pass judgment without . . . understanding their experience.[11]

Finding Help

Until the mid-1970s, very little help was available for suicide survivors. But when experts who specialized in suicide prevention began to realize that those most likely to kill themselves were the survivors, they suddenly took an interest in them. As a result, prevention centers began to offer counseling services to those left behind.

Next, a few survivors decided to follow a national trend in the 1970s and start self-help groups. They established organizations, such as Survivors of Suicide, held meetings, and invited other survivors to join them, to share their feelings with people who really understood their pain. Some of these meetings were presided over by survivors; others were led by mental health professionals.

In 1980, Survivors of Suicide held its first national conference. It was followed by many more. These meetings drew attention to the issue of suicide and enabled leaders of the conferences to educate the public about self-inflicted death. Leaders at the meetings also created a network of support services for survivors.

As a result, today survivors can receive help no matter where they live. They can call local suicide hot lines or contact clergymen, school counselors, or funeral directors. Social workers at hospitals and in clinics can provide information and help as well. No one has to struggle with his or her feelings alone. There is life after death, and there are people willing to help survivors find it.

Helping a Survivor

Because all of us sometime in our lives are likely to know someone who committed suicide, it is important to know how to comfort the survivors. Below are some suggestions from grief counselors.

1. Show concern. Attend the wake, visitation, funeral, or memorial service. A public show of support is important to grief-stricken survivors. If possible, offer your condolences at the service. A handshake, a hug, or a simple "I'm so sorry," means more than you can imagine at such a time. If you can't attend a service, send a card, call the family, or make a contribution to a memorial fund.

2. Listen. Listen. Listen. Survivors need to vent their feelings. To do this, they need to talk about what happened, and they need people who will listen—and not judge—what they say.

3. Offer to run errands. Sometimes survivors are too numb to do everyday errands. Volunteer to pick up groceries, take them to appointments, or to bring friends to the house to visit.

4. Check on their physical well-being. Are they eating properly? Are they getting exercise? Do they need to see a doctor?

5. When appropriate, help them find counseling.

Chapter Notes

Chapter 1. Death in the Headlines

1. Roger Cohen, "Cobain-Inspired Suicides Unnerve French Town," *Milwaukee Journal Sentinel*, June 1, 1997, p. 8A.

2. Ibid.

3. "Polite Student Plays Trick to Die," *Milwaukee Journal Sentinel*, November 18, 1997, p. 13A.

4. Meg Jones, "Man Critical After Being Shot by Police," *Milwaukee Journal Sentinel*, November 25, 1997, pp. 1B, 4B.

5. "When Rage Explodes," *Milwaukee Journal Sentinel*, December 20, 1997, pp. 1A, 8A.

6. Laura Dolce, *Suicide*. (New York: Chelsea House Publishers, 1992), p. 13.

Chapter 2. Suicide in the Past

1. George Howe Colt, *The Enigma of Suicide*. (New York: Summit Books, 1991), pp. 129–130.

2. Ibid., pp. 130–131.

3. Johann W. Von Goethe, *The Sorrows of Young Werther*, ed. David E. Wellbery (New York: Suhrkamp Verlag, 1988), pp. 37, 54, 62, 85–86.

Chapter 3. Who Commits Suicide?

1. Centers for Disease Control and Prevention, National Center for Health Statistics, "Suicide," *Fastats*, May 28, 1998, <http://www.cdc.gov/nchswww/fastats/suicide.htm> (September 15, 1998); National Institute of Mental Health, "Suicide Fact Sheet," *Suicide Research Consortium*, July 1, 1998, <http://www.nimh.nih.gov/research/suicide/htm> (September 15, 1998).

2. Laura Dolce, *Suicide* (New York: Chelsea House Publishers, 1992), pp. 13–14.

3. Nancy J. Osgood, *Suicide in Later Life: Recognizing the Warning Signs* (New York: Lexington Books, 1992), p. 13.

4. George Howe Colt, *The Enigma of Suicide* (New York: Summit Books, 1991), p. 256.

5. Ibid., p. 255.

6. Ibid., p. 248.

7. Gary Remafedi, "Homosexual Teens Are at High Risk for Suicide," in *Suicide: Opposing Viewpoints*, ed. Tamara Roleff (San Diego: Greenhaven Press, 1998), p. 63.

8. Gary Remafedi, ed., *Death by Denial: Studies of Suicide in Gay and Lesbian Teenagers* (Boston: Alyson Publications, 1994), p. 17.

Chapter 4. Why?

1. Leslie Laurence, "Time to Level With Teen-age Girls," *Oshkosh Northwestern*, January 10, 1995, p. D2.

2. Vernon R. Weide, *Sibling Abuse: Hidden Physical, Emotional, and Sexual Trauma* (Lexington, Mass.: D. C. Heath and Company, 1990), p. 111.

3. George Howe Colt, *The Enigma of Suicide* (New York: Summit Books, 1991), p. 203.

4. Ibid.

5. John Chiles, *Teenage Depression and Suicide* (New York: Chelsea House Publishers, 1986), p. 47.

6. Laura Dolce, *Suicide* (New York: Chelsea House Publishers, 1992), p. 53.

7. Herbert Hendin, *Suicide in America* (New York: W. W. Norton & Company, 1982), p. 60.

8. Colt, p. 49.

9. Dolce, p. 30.

10. "Suicide Rate Leaps Among Black Teen-agers," *Oshkosh Northwestern*, March 20, 1998, p. A4.

11. Nancy J. Osgood, *Suicide in Later Life: Recognizing the Warning Signs* (New York: Lexington Books, 1992), p. 17.

12. Ibid.

13. Evan Thomas, "The Next Level," *Time*, April 7, 1997, pp. 28–35.

14. Ritch C. Savin-Williams, "Verbal and Physical Abuse as Stressors in the Lives of Lesbian, Gay Male, and Bisexual Youths," *Suicide*, ed. Robert E. Long (New York: H. W. Wilson, 1995), p. 32.

15. Ibid., p. 33.

16. Ibid., pp. 36–39.

17. Colt, p. 260.

18. Don Feder, "A Fabricated Crisis," in *Suicide: Opposing Viewpoints*, ed. Tamara Roleff (San Diego: Greenhaven Press, 1998), p. 68.

Chapter 5. How?

1. Christopher Scanlan, "Guns in the Home Contribute to Teen Suicide," *Suicide: Opposing Viewpoints*, ed. Tamara Roleff (San Diego: Greenhaven Press, 1998), p. 52.

2. Laura Dolce, *Suicide* (New York: Chelsea House Publishers, 1992), p. 16.

3. Scanlan, p. 53.

4. Dolce, p. 16.

5. Bernard Frankel and Rachel Kranz, *Straight Talk About Teenage Suicide* (New York: Facts On File, 1994), pp. 83–84.

6. Jerry Johnston, *Why Suicide?* (Nashville: Oliver-Nelson Books, 1987), p. 9.

7. George Howe Colt, *The Enigma of Suicide* (New York: Summit Books, 1991), p. 240.

Chapter 6. To Save a Life

1. George Howe Colt, *The Enigma of Suicide* (New York: Summit Books, 1991), p. 295.

2. Ibid., pp. 282–283.

3. Bernard Frankel and Rachel Franz, *Straight Talk About Teenage Suicide* (New York: Facts On File, 1994), pp. 88–89.

4. Ibid., p. 92.

Chapter 7. The Right to Die

1. "Readers Voice Their Views on Right to Die," *Oshkosh Northwestern*, October 13, 1997, p. D3.

2. Michael Betzold, "The Selling of Doctor Death," *The New Republic*, May 26, 1997, p. 23.

3. Ibid., p. 26.

4. David Goodman, "Kevorkian Proposes Transplant," *Milwaukee Journal Sentinel*, June 8, 1998, p. 8A.

5. David Van Biema, "Death's Door Left Ajar," *Time*, July 7, 1997, p. 30.

6. "Court Passes on Assisted Suicide Law," *Milwaukee Journal Sentinel*, October 15, 1997, p. 1A.

7. "Doctor-Assisted Suicide Law Gets First Known Use," *Milwaukee Journal Sentinel*, March 26, 1998, p. 11A.

Chapter 8. Life After Death

1. Christopher Lukas and Henry M. Seiden, *Silent Grief: Living in the Wake of Suicide* (New York: Charles Scribner's Sons, 1987), p. 19.

2. Ibid., p. 32.

3. Ibid.

4. "Readers Reply: Suicide Devastating to Survivors," *Oshkosh Northwestern*, July 6, 1997, p. F5.

5. Ibid.

6. George Howe Colt, *The Enigma of Suicide* (New York: Summit Books, 1991), p. 431.

7. Lukas and Seiden, p. 111.

8. Ibid., p. 16.

9. Gary Rummler, "Life After Death," *Milwaukee Journal Sentinel*, August 3, 1997, pp. 1L, 4L.

10. Ibid.

11. Jonathan Smith, "How Dare You Judge My Mom's Decision to Die," *Milwaukee Journal Sentinel*, June 22, 1997, pp. 1J, 2J.

Further Reading

Ayer, Eleanor. *Teen Suicide: Is It Too Painful to Grow Up?* New York: Twenty-First Century Books, 1995.

Campbell, Wanda. *Suicide: Reason for Living.* London: PPI Publishing, 1995.

Flanders, Stephen A. *Suicide.* New York: Facts On File, 1991.

Gay, Kathlyn. *The Right to Die: Public Controversy, Private Matter.* Brookfield, Conn.: Millbrook Press, 1993.

Hyde, Margaret O., and Elizabeth H. Forsyth. *Suicide.* 3rd ed. Danbury, Conn.: Franklin Watts, 1991.

Leder, Jane M. *Dead Serious: A Book for Teenagers about Teenage Suicide.* New York: Simon & Schuster Children's, 1987.

Lewis, Cynthia Copeland. *Teen Suicide: Too Young to Die.* Springfield, N.J.: Enslow Publishers, 1994.

McGuire, Leslie. *Suicide.* Vero Beach, Fla.: Rourke Corporation, 1990.

Steele, Bill. *Surviving the Epidemic of Suicide.* London: PPI Publishing, 1994.

Walker, Richard. *A Right to Die?* Danbury, Conn.: Franklin Watts Incorporated, 1997.

Woog, Adam. *Suicide.* San Diego: Lucent Books, 1996.

Internet Addresses

American Association of Suicidology

<http://www.cyberpsych.org/aas/index.htm>

Provides reports and information on suicide rates and suicide prevention.

American Foundation for Suicide Prevention (AFSP)

<http://www.afsp.org>

AFSP funds research, education, and treatment programs. Its Web site provides facts about assisted suicide, youth suicide, and the relationships between AIDS, depression, neurobiology, and suicide.

Suicide Information and Education Centre

<http://www.siec.ca>

This Canadian organization maintains an expansive library on suicide, provides answers to frequently asked questions, and lists links to many other sites.

Suicide Prevention Advocacy Network (SPAN)

<http://www.spanusa.org>

This nonprofit organization is dedicated to the creation of an effective national suicide prevention strategy. It gives information on suicide prevention and suicide rates.

Index